A MORE EXCELLENT WAY

FAMILY GUIDE TO ACADEMIC SUCCESS
AND COLLEGE PLANNING

TORRY A. JOHNSON

Copyright © 2021 by Torry A. Johnson

All rights reserved. No part of this book may be used or reproduced in any manner whatsoever without the express written permission of the author except for the use of brief quotations in a book review.

Printed in the United States of America

ISBN: 978-1-7358701-4-4

First Printing, 2021

Cover by: Kendra Powell – Inek Graphics

JayMedia Publishing

Laurel, MD 20708

www.publishing.jaymediagroup.net

Table of Contents

Introduction | v

1. Structure | 1
2. They've Got to Learn How to Write | 4
3. Get to the Library | 7
4. Homework is for Students, Not for Parents | 9
5. Create the Right Atmosphere | 13
6. Effective Study Habits | 17
7. Test Taking | 20
8. Communication Skills | 24
9. Giving Back & Serving Others | 27
10. Extracurricular Activities: Clubs, Jobs & Sports | 31
11. Own Your GPA | 35

12. Standardized Tests | 39

13. Media Consumption | 43

14. Celebrate Student Accomplishments | 47

15. Graduation Party | 52

16. Majors and Minors | 57

17. College Tours vs. College Visits | 62

18. Selecting Your School | 68

19. College Affordability | 70

20. Scholarships | 75

21. Save Early & Often | 81

22. Paying for College | 87

23. Consider the Investment in Your Student | 91

24. Our Family Strategy for No Student Loans | 96

25. Students Must be Active in the Process | 101

26. Don't Just Survive, Thrive | 104

Epilogue: PAID IN FULL | 107

Introduction

How did I come to write this book? Who says that I know any more than the next person? Each are valid questions. Every one of us has been blessed with skills, abilities or talents. My eldest coined this phrase: "God-Given Gifts" when she was much younger as GGG. Inevitably, if and when, we tap into this intersection where passion and destiny meet, we can do some extraordinary things and impact lives in the process.

For me, while definitely not the greatest student of all time, I have been fortunate to have a gift when it comes to understanding the demands of educational pursuits, how to synthesize academic messages so that students and families can understand and follow. Furthermore, I have mentored, tutored, coached, worked, coordinated, programmed and advised in one academic capacity or another for non-profit organizations, government agencies, religious groups and friends/family for over 25 years.

In the business world, they call that "real world" experience. Seen it. Tried it. Done it. And in the end, I have had the opportunity to model it for others. I have spent time working in afterschool and weekend enrichment programs designed to motivate, invigorate and challenge students beyond the traditional classroom. Over the years, I have also championed local spelling bees, adult reading, GED and SAT prep classes. The beauty of my background is that what I didn't experience, I made contacts in the more formal academic arenas. These relationships with teachers, professors, deans, academic & board chairs, faculty, chancellors, presidents and principals have allowed me access to a world of academic insight that I would have never imaged or envisioned. I am very appreciative of these colleagues and their expertise.

Over the years I have seen my share of academic successes, failures and all the vicissitudes that fall in between those bookends. I recall the dreaded group projects of middle and high school fondly (or not so fondly). Trying to pull together friends, frenemies and co-conspirators for the purpose of completing a joint effort. Oftentimes one or more of the parties didn't pull their own weight. Navigating that tricky terrain helped me to develop skills of negotiation, compromise, true partnership and collaboration. You may think these aren't necessary for academic success, but I beg to differ. My aim is to hopefully impact or convey these key points repeatedly throughout this text.

During my earlier years, I had the chance to volunteer at local/neighboring schools as a mentor or tutor. Giving back (discussed in later chapters) to others had been a practice of mine since my high school and college days. Tutoring didn't mean that I was smarter than others in a given subject matter; it meant that I knew how to convey the essence of the lesson so that others could "get it" and have their own "ah-ha" moments going forward. Having worked with rural, urban and suburban students, I can say that every demographic of student has some area that they want to do better in: reading language arts, math, writing and the list goes on. As kids get older, bad habits can get worse; new difficulties can manifest and the ability to engage new tools (this concept is addressed later) to aide them in appropriately (re)framing challenging concepts, problems and assignments which become increasingly more difficult to solve.

The notion of hard work should not be synonymous for impossible to do, but more of a call to greater vigilance, better focus, a heightened sense of deliberateness in the way(s) one should proceed to be the aforementioned successful. Let me be clear that I am NOT an educator by state and federal standards. My knowledge comes from consistent and repeated engagement with educators, master teachers, Einstein Fellows, students (K-20), test prep centers, and families trying to help their student remedy an area that is not allowing them to be their best self. This is where I can help. That has always been my hope and prayer.

Before we get into the nuts and bolts of this book, I want to finally say that when and where appropriate, I have looked for anecdotal remedies and authentic examples to assist in driving home my points. By no means is this book exhaustive, hence the brevity that these mere pages represent. With so many families asking me to share what we have used in my household, with my family, I am pouring it out to you. Please use this as one of many resources. There are so many additional links, help aides and places for more support, encouragement and information. My desire is that this book begins a conversation about what academic success does and does not look like.

Equally importa nt is that our foray into funding college (without loans) will be chocked full of Johnson experiences - pitfalls, snafus, successes and high plateaus - all for your benefit. Learn from us. Learn what to do or what not to do. Learn what might be good for you or not. Let's learn from each other. Feel free to reach out to me on social media (Instagram or Facebook) to address questions, thoughts and purposefully to add many more voices that can give balance and depth to our discussion topic.

So, here we go. I am opening my head and my heart. Take what you will. Question what I say. Argue with my rationale. Disagree with my approach. But whatever you do, don›t turn a blind eye or deaf ear to finding help and guidance for you and your students - that would be most tragic. Enjoy. Let's enter in and prepare to go deeper.

Structure

Routine: bath, pajamas, bedtime story, prayers and lights out. Repeat. As I think back to the time when our kids were much younger, around 4 to 6 years old, we made a concerted effort to establish structure. How could you not? With three kids, absent a structure, you're creating a recipe for mini-disasters. When you set order, things tend to fall more in line. You also can tell what is out of order and that is equally important. While these challenges are altogether correctable, it is important to start out on sure footing. Structure does not just apply to the bedtime routine. Consider any part of the day, week, etc. that would necessitate a plan with consistency. That could be exam/testing weeks, major project or presentation prep or anything of that elk. Just remember that any matter that one wants to get good at, will require planning, practice and repetition. Your family unit - especially your students - need it. By creating the framework, your kids/students will be able to "plug and play". Some young people are able to find their way more readily when a good foundation is laid for them. Absent this, some will flail about unnecessarily. No need to waste that kind of time and energy. Help everyone by setting lines of demarcation and sticking to them. This will reap dividends for your kids as they mature and ultimately find themselves facing (young) adulthood. Along with structure, I want to pivot and say that order and boundaries let your students know limits that help them function at their best.

Proper rest fits right in here with the others. As a parent, one of our jobs is to make certain that our kids receive adequate rest and that we - the parents - establish the bedtime, not the other way around. All too often I hear parents say, "Well, they just weren't tired enough." Really? In the Johnson household, at approximately 7:00pm-7:30pm, the bedtime routine would begin for our three little ones. Remember to set a schedule early in your child's lives - homework, meals, bedtime - it is all about the routine. Obviously, I am making this a really abbreviated process to get the point across, but at the end of the day, parents need to set the tone/structure, build it early enough and then fill it with good stuff that you ultimately want to see in your children.

I understand that with younger children, multiple siblings and the like, the schedule may not run as smooth as you want initially; but the aim is that your entire household will begin to see a pattern and conform to it. The noise level and energy in the house should start down-shifting shortly after dinner. You might be saying to yourself, *But my kids still haven't finished their homework.* (See Chapter 4 on Homework). There are some caveats which are dependent upon the age and grade level of the kids, and also whether or not it they are on winter or summer breaks. I am not that rigid! Just remember - structure has to be established, so that your whole family can function at an optimal level. Think of the concept of trial and error. Figure out what works best for your family. Ask your friends and family members – someone that your respect – how their household is ordered or organized. Just like in sewing, use a pattern until you can go free-hand.

They've Got to Learn How to Write

Your student should know or learn how to write essays, paragraphs, short stories, and more. *Oh boy. Here he goes saying my baby doesn't know how to write.* Don›t blame me, I didn't take handwriting out of school. Knowing how to write has next to nothing to do with penmanship, but far more to do with the ability to convey one's thoughts in a clear and logical manner so that others can follow. The reason we spend so much time in the formative years of child's development teaching them letters, words, phonics and reading is not just to check the proverbial box. It is intended to aid us in conversation and clearly articulating what is on our minds. While I get that only 7% [*Mehrabian,*

Albert, Silent Messages, 1971] of our communication is actually verbal (words only) and 38% vocal (including tone of voice, inflection, and other sounds), building a capacity for writing and doing that well is a benefit, if not a necessity.

Your child or student will have to convey numerous actions and thoughts, such as: letting people know what they did on summer break, how they felt when their favorite show was cancelled and quite possibly how the Iliad and the Odyssey conveyed a sense of nobility without hindering the writer's voice. You won't just be able to say it. You will have to write it. And my friends, your student's ability (or inability) to write will speak volumes about them, and possibly you – think about that.

So, you say, *Torry, how do we foster good writing while my son or daughter is so young?* You start by getting them to read, and having them read often. Then, diversifying what they read. Then, having them read things that challenge their thinking and eventually their ideologies. *Whoa! Stop right there. I thought the aim was to help our young ones and here you are talking about possibly going against what we have taught our impressionable young ones* [sarcasm intended]. Why, yes I am. I am saying to start your kids on Little Golden Book classics like, *The Little Red Hen* or *The Pokie Little Puppy* or Dr. Seuss. But you will have to push past the "wocket in my pocket" to ensure that your youngster gets a firm grip on reality before introducing the fantastical and enchanting stories that will form some of their most exciting reading years. The greatest way to inform one's writing mind, in my humble opinion, is to constantly introduce multiple styles of writing that they can consume. In addition to quality books, there are comic books, graphic novels, periodicals, magazines, newspapers, pamphlets, journals, and dictionaries, to name a few.

Get to the Library

One of the greatest gifts a parent can give their child is a free library card. I remember going to the library where I grew up in New Carrollton, MD and getting my first card. I had to fill out an application, and then I received this plastic card with my signature on the back. Wow... I was now on the loose in the library to read, reserve and check out all kinds of media, books on tape, music CDs (HA!) - you name it. Fast forward 20 years and my wife begins to take our children to that very same library. Every week or so she would pack the kids up and head off to the library. They enjoyed "story time", they loved roaming around their respective sections and locating books that interested them and most importantly, they loved checking out THEIR book selections with THEIR own library cards. Of course, as parents we still had the final say on selection, but they got the first pass.

Over the years, the kids developed their own rhythm in the library. They had a particular way of how they selected books. What mood were they in during a particular season of life? What were their interest areas at the time? How did that play into their book choices? Ultimately, it is not only that you gain a library card, but you also gain a love for reading and all that it brings. As a parent, I liked to make sure that my kids initially read the books on the public school summer reading list. After that, we would peruse the private school lists. Trust me, there was never a time when there wasn't something to read.

I will put a plug here. Parents, this is a great opportunity for you to shepherd them through the process of learning to enjoy books and reading. If you push them to go to the library, grab a book for yourself and be the example that they need to facilitate their love of reading. Or you might say, my child is a pre-teen and doesn't like to read. I would say to make it a requirement. Start your student off with picture books and gradually decrease the number of pictures over time. Books on tape are also a great starting place until they are ready to read on their own. In this digital age, the library is still a critical part of student development. While there are e-books and other sorts of media now, continue to encourage the role of the library and the real or virtual accessing of books.

Homework is for Students, Not for Parents

Now that we are friends, I feel that we can go deeper. Repeat after me: "Homework is for students; not for parents." Say it like you mean it this time. Your hearts are in the right place, but the execution is askew. Let's look at this example:

> A family has two children, ages 9 & 15. Each day the parents frantically pour over websites trying to learn how to do their kid's assignments before they arrive home that evening. The frustration mounts because they are not sure if the online approach meshes with the Common Core framework taught at the kid's school. To make matters

worse, the kids do not have a good handle on the math either. Their notes were sketchy, at best, and coupled with their parent's vague comprehension of the problem set, the evening has begun to spiral down.

This is a critical point to understand and embrace. Your child's teacher is not trying to figure out if you, as the parent, can complete the assignment. On the contrary, the homework is designed to give the student a chance to practice, with repetition, the concepts generally addressed in the classroom. Practice will make perfect.

Torry, you are out of sorts again. Don't you know that we parents need to help our kids with the homework, else it won't get done? We need to attempt to develop answers, so we can give that much needed assistance. I hear you parents, especially the new age, internet savvy, helicopter parents. You want a teacher to believe that your student came up with the fossil fuel project all by themselves without the help of their coal executive dad or that your student typed all four pages of their book report, given the syllabus asked for two handwritten pages.

Many of you may have been nodding your heads in mutual acknowledgment having gone through similar situations at your own kitchen table. Let me offer a

Homework is for Students, Not for Parents

different look at the same scenario.

> Parents are aware their children have had some difficulty with the recent math assignments. They ask the youngsters to pull out their notebooks and the corresponding homework text and/or book. The parents ask them to review their notes and any practice problems that give insight into the homework. The parents aim to create an appropriate environment for homework to be accomplished. The parents then assign some time for students to work independently.

Any questions? What, you thought there was something else? Nope. You say, "What if they get stuck and cannot get through the problem?" I say, encourage them to carefully reread the practice problem and the notes, and then attempt to complete the problem by writing out each of the steps. If they still cannot solve the problem, have them circle that problem (or the type of problem) which is giving the most challenge. This way the teacher can be alerted to issue. Next step - move on to next problem or assignment. No need spending excessive time on something the student doesn't understand. Academic instruction of the material, at its core, is a function of the school system. Let the teachers do that. We can support, augment, foster & undergird, but generally speaking, we are NOT the educator in this case. Stop trying to be what you are not.

Will this be hard for you to do? Yes, especially if you have been providing so much hands-on, over engagement with your student. Both you and the student are accustomed to this method. You might even notice your children anticipating your help to the point that they don't try very long at all. They ask, parent swoops in, everyone takes on their role and the student doesn't get to exercise their academic muscles as they should.

Are you wondering if this lesson only applies to older kids, say in middle or high school? It follows for students of all age groups. As the child develops and matures, we should endeavor to aid them in growing with respect to self-reliance and independence. This does not mean we abandon them entirely. Oh no! On the contrary, you should empower your students with tools that allow them to properly assess their academic challenge and then to engage the requisite resource(s) for successful resolution.

Let us leave this topic for a moment (we will revisit) because I don't want you to get stuck and tune me out going forward. Some of this book is intended to cause you to think differently about how you are supporting or enabling your child academically.

Create the Right Atmosphere

What is the most conducive environment for your student to thrive and excel in? It is the place where they get the following in ample doses: love, attention, structure, encouragement, support and freedom to be autonomous. My hope is that your home embodies all of that and then some. If it does not, then you have time to fix that or create another space where that can be fostered. While I speak to physical changes in this next paragraph, it is important to have safe spaces, judgment free spaces, uplifting spaces and so on. Some people may not be able to institute physical changes, but the mood can be transferred by working on some of these previously referenced items.

Part of creating the right atmosphere is tied to the proper conditions. Is the area free from clutter? Is there a lot of foot traffic and noise that could possibly cause the students to lose focus or be easily distracted? Something that many parents and guardians forget is whether or not there is adequate lighting in the space. Can the student make out all of the verbiage on the page, computer or agenda book? These are all very important. Some people might be wondering if having music or headphones on is appropriate. Good question! My answer here would be, "It depends". While it is important to set boundaries and guidelines, it is equally important to allow some free space for your child to attempt some things on their own. Allow some latitude in music being playing (not overly loud), or perhaps via headphones. See if it takes longer to complete the homework or assignment with the music playing or not playing. You will have to do some testing and assessing. The other key determinant is the success or lack thereof, with respect to the student's grades, marks and overall academic prowess.

Give your student a chance to weigh in on any changes or modifications to the approach. This empowers them and lets them know that you have confidence in their decision making. Remember, we are also growing them in terms of their independent thinking. With

Create the Right Atmosphere 15

my kids, I have a daughter that loves all types of music, and she could sometimes be found listening to classical music when studying. My oldest sometimes had complete silence, and yet my son moved between sitting, lounging on the bed, playing music with earbuds, without headphones, etc. The options are not infinite, but there are sundry ways to accomplish this goal. Have fun with your children. Switch things up. Show them that you are interested, and you are willing to make adjustments for their benefit. Both of you will appreciate it.

Kids that cannot get proper rest, adequate nutrition, and some dedicated work space (bedroom, kitchen table, desk, etc.) will find themselves constantly at a disadvantage when it comes to settling into their academic "zone" for success. You may say that for whatever reason your student doesn't have the requisite or desired space, then I say, find it or create it. Let them visit a local library or bookstore where they can have a few hours without constant interruption and/or noise. Within your house, see if there is any space that can be used as a dedicated "homework" zone once the student is home from school.

By starting this practice at home, the aim is that your student will begin to make adjustments to how they accomplish their studying, work, projects and thus, how they thrive academically. When all is said and done, your son or daughter is setting the tone for what they will do when they reach middle/high school and even higher education.

Effective Study Habits

If you do not know this by now, many of the concepts mentioned in this book are interconnected. We just talked briefly about creating the right environment for success. Why? So that we can properly implement effective study habits. Remember that my ideas are not an exhaustive list, but they hopefully will provide suggestions and possible paths forward.

In order to effectively study one must have the requisite materials for studying: textbook or reading material, previous notes, assignment, additional resources, web sites, teacher handouts, etc.

Let us stick a pin here and stress the importance of making sure your student is accurately capturing assignments, problem sets and the like from the teacher. According to Woody Allen, if "80% of success is just showing up", then writing down the correct assignment is a similar percentage of the academic fight. You would not believe how many times I have tutored students that either copied the wrong problem set and/or did not verify the assignment with the teacher before leaving school. Here is where you can work with your student. Here are a few tips:

- Check your student's journal or homework log early in the school year.
- See if it lines up with what the teacher has posted online or confirm via email.
- Once you see a consistent pattern of 100% accuracy, no need to keep checking up.

Since we have already discussed homework, I want us to focus more so on creating good study habits. Make sure that studying is viewed as an action separate and distinct from homework. Students should review notes, re-read difficult or confusing sections, and re-work problems or concepts that still pose a challenge. All of these habits help build confidence and mastery, so that the student can "show and tell" when it comes time for exams, tests and oral presentations.

One other word, please make sure you (or your student) have a couple of classmates names and current contact information. This is good for bouncing ideas, verifying assignments, comparing notes and recovery of missed items while out for sick or travel days. Your student should function as a resource in the same manner for their peers. This will help develop collaboration and future teaming skills.

Make sure that adequate time is being spent on studying. You will know by their grades and scores if there is not. Ask your student to explain their approach (if old enough). Younger kids should follow the model that their parents or guardians have enacted (or modify things that you have hopefully learned here).

Test Taking

Hopefully you've noticed that we are building upon concepts or ideas. So, it is natural that this test taking chapter would follow the effective study habits chapter. Test taking starts with preparation or the lack thereof. Remember to start with questioning how your student is getting their information. What will the test be covering? Always have them review the general scope of the subject matter that is fair game on the test. Your student should then look for the corresponding notes that line up with the test prep material. This is often a great way for them to re-familiarize themselves with the key concepts, approaches, strategies, etc. They should take the time to highlight, jot down additional questions or "a-ha's" that they may uncover during the review.

Another consideration is to pull together two or three classmates to video chat or have an in-person study session with. This is a good way to engage different perspectives and thoughts. If the student only hears their own voice, they may be missing out on other critically important vantage points. Their classmates may have looked at the passage or assignment in an entirely different way. Please understand me, I don't mean for them to abandon their own thinking and migrate to that of their classmate. No, what I do mean is that they should value and get multiple voices upon which to make good test prep decisions.

The tried-and-true approach, if possible, is to have a study group in person. Maybe this can be accomplished afterschool and coordinated with the teacher, or the students could reserve some time/space at the neighborhood library. All of those vacant study rooms are waiting for your student. Now you might ask, *how does one structure the test review session?* Delegate. Look to split the test content amongst the students. Let one handle chapters X-Z, another would pull together some difficult homework problems and another could discuss any possible test review that the teacher provided. The aim is to get everyone involved. Aside from focusing on the test at hand, this experience will give your student a great opportunity to work in teams, learn responsibility and present their portion of the material. This is a critical skill and not one that will go without testing and proving throughout life (college, work teams, etc.).

One last thing on test preparation and studying - do not wait for the last minute to begin your preparation, especially when it comes to difficult material and/or items that have proven challenging for you in the past. The worse thing in the world to do is to attempt to cram loosely understood concepts and content into one's brain at the last moment. Trust me, it will not stay there long. You are begging for confusion and mix-ups. Give yourself adequate time to prepare. *Note: if there is a pop-quiz or test, the routine studying plan that we discussed earlier in the book would best be applied.*

A rarely applied technique that is critical for sustained academic success is proper review of a completed and graded test/exam. Unless the student received 100% on their test – not including extra credit – meaning they got every element of the test correct, they have an opportunity to go back and redo the questions or problems that they missed some points on. Especially with math - make sure to work the problem out in its entirety. Each step is vital for your student's comprehension and future mastery of the subject. This process should be repeated for each graded assignment. Parents you will need to be on this action step because your student will not want to do it. More so, when the results were really high (80% or higher) or really low (60% or lower). Both extremities will make your student stronger than they were prior to taking the test. Remember, this chapter is about "test taking", not grade getting. We will discuss grades, grade point average (GPA) and the like soon enough.

Communication Skills

8

How does your student communicate overall? How does your student communicate with you? With their friends? Interesting questions, I know. Would you say that your student does a relatively good job at conveying their thoughts? Are they better or worse when it comes to speaking up for themselves in public? Orally or in writing? How is their grammar? Do they talk in "text" speak? Do you find yourself trying to understand their slang? Welcome to the wonderful world of communication. We will pull several of these questions apart, so that we can speak to each of these matters separately (although you will definitely see some overlap).

How does your student communicate?

Well. Enough to get along. Poorly. Not sure. Trust me, I hear you. Especially, as your children get closer to their teenage years, you will be reexamining this question again and again. If your student wants something from you or another, how is that request made? Making sure that kids understand that respect in their communication is crucial. Respectful dialogue which honors those in authority, acknowledges differing viewpoints and allows for measured discourse is always in order. Ensuring that our young people know how to voice their opinion is necessary not only for academics, but also for life. Your household can prove a great training ground on how to properly make requests/demands in addition to learning how to deal with dissent and disappointment.

How does your student convey their own thoughts?

This is often exemplified in the arts like poetry, singing, rapping and art. While I firmly promote the core subjects, it is critical to encourage your student/child to express their own thoughts in constructive ways. Our second oldest daughter is a great writer. She even represented her school and county in a poetry competition in high school. The arts are becoming outlets for young people.

There can also be an academic style component to communication - the way in which your student comports themselves with respect to their coursework. It can also include how they engage in the classroom and how they "flow" with their classmates. Are they the leader on projects? Do they like to add the flare for presentations? Do they have a penchant for handling the underlying research? All are key roles that allow them to shine.

Is your student finding their own voice?

This can be shown in the above descriptions, or they can be exhibited in extracurricular endeavors like: sports, journaling/blogging, instruments, graphic design, game development or others. The opportunities are quite numerous. As parents, this is where we should encourage, watch and be ready to pivot – sometimes at a moment's notice. Ultimately, our role is to cultivate, introduce and support them.

9

Giving Back & Serving Others

As for me and my house, we will serve. Serve who, you might ask. That's rather easy. Whoever needs to be served - kids, seniors, schools, causes, you name it. There are ways that our kids can and should serve. This was a fundamental way in how I was raised and what I modeled in front of my children. Tutoring is a way that I choose to give back; my wife does it by working with teenage girls and women.

You can feed the hungry, give toys to a hospital, provide clothes to a shelter, or participate in a book drive. These are but a few examples of ways that your student can get the attention off of themselves and onto someone that needs assistance.

Serving others also allows your student to cultivate some more latent or dormant skills - cooperation, teamwork, humility, sticking to a task and following another person's lead. Let me share a quick example of my childhood:

> Our local church served food to the homeless in the neighborhood. My dad would wake me early, so that we could get to the wholesale market and pick-up chicken, vegetables and associated items to bring to the cooks that would prepare soups and meals for our guests.

Helping individuals that were less fortunate than I was reminded me of how blessed we were and that I shouldn't take it for granted. What I didn't know then – as a kid less than 10 years old - was that volunteering and serving was becoming a part of my makeup. I could help serve meals, read to senior citizens, tutor students – the list goes on and on. Additionally, these experiences can help keep your child's ego in check. The "me, me, me" complex periodically needs to be reined in. Giving back is a productive way of helping develop them in that area.

You might be asking yourself: *how will I get my student to do this?* You will have to take them unless they are part of Boy Scouts or Girl Scouts or some other Fraternity/

Giving Back & Serving Others

Sorority mentoring program. Your school, library or church will also know where the real help is needed.

I believe that middle school is a great time to introduce the concept, maybe around the holidays when you can visit a nursing home and deliver baskets and/or sing carols. Give your student something tangible to do: pack baskets or sign all the Christmas cards. Additionally, have kids invite a friend. Remember we want to show them that life is not always about them; there are others to consider.

Quiet as kept, I didn't care much for leaving super early on Saturday mornings and heading to the wholesale market to buy food for the "Feed the Hungry" program at my local church growing up as a kid. It was tough (in my mind), yet the more I went, the more I connected with the people and the cause.

While I still enjoy working with food servicing programs, my passion is working with students and families around academic matters. Serving can help you find what you might eventually love to do, whether you get paid or not. Tutoring in college helped put me on a path to my lifelong objective of programming for academic success in families. While volunteering, your son or daughter may be sowing seeds in their future career field.

Volunteering has got to be more than just a holiday season occasion though. You must model it before the next generation. Your local school, church or municipality can be an awesome kick starter. Through the local scouts in our areas, our kids sorted groceries at a food bank, provided participant support at charity walks/events, donated toys for children in the hospital. Sometimes the kids would go with groups and other times they were solo. As my kids moved into college, the level of volunteering grew to causes and charities that most interested them as individuals. You get the point. It is important not only for them, but for society. Show them how to give back.

10

Extracurricular Activities: Clubs, Jobs & Sports

"All work and no play makes Jack a dull boy." [Howell, James, *Proverbs*, 1659] Many of you may have heard this phrase growing up. With a slightly different spin, we might say that absent extra-curricular activities Jack/Jill may seem to be a bland, one-dimensional student. Please don't take this statement to mean that EVERY child should be engaged in ALL three activities (clubs, jobs & sports). On the contrary, I feel that the majority of students will only be able to handle one additional element outside of their academic pursuits.

Let's be clear, education is why students go to school, especially in K-12. As your student gets closer to high school, they need to begin a process of diversifying their interests. They need to find things outside of class/homework to occupy their time and their mind. These extra-curricular activities can serve to balance a student, round out their character, and even give insight into future career & social paths. Let's unpack each activity to get a better look at them.

Clubs - those after school or in the community activities that allow your student to meet other students, rally around a particular cause or event and quite possibly hone your leadership and follower-ship skills. Most high school students should be able to find at least one club to be a part of. As I mentioned socialization skills can be addressed - getting to know more students outside of the classroom is always a plus! You might also include your local Boy/Girl Scout Troop, church choir or mentoring program.

Added bonuses are that your student can learn time management and serving of others. Clubs also serve as a nice way for other school or community organizations and their leaders a chance to get to know your student outside of the classroom. Think about competitions such as Spelling Bee, Science Fair, ROTC, cheerleading, etc. I believe that you get my point. Have fun while learning to be engaged with team-based events and activities. **Bonus**

point: if you don't find the club of your interest, think about what might be missing and seek to create a club yourself or with some of your friends.

Jobs are another item to consider outside of school. My kids are probably frowning at me right now because although I maintained a job through most of high school and college, I only supported our kids getting jobs or internships during the summer in high school and only part-time beginning junior year of college. The academic challenges are so significant and one's ability to perform at a high level directly correlates with academic success and inevitably merit awards and scholarships. Each family will have to weigh this area and figure out what is most suitable for your household. I grew up working at Pizza Hut and Giant Food while in high school. It allowed me to get out of the house in the evenings and weekends while also covering my graduation expenses and some of my freshman year in college. While I learned a lot and was somewhat independent, financially, I tended to procrastinate on assignments/papers because I was really focused on the "almighty dollar". **Bonus point**: be careful and know what the intended outcome should be. Any time that the school work suffers or students are oversleeping, not addressing things at home properly, etc. ---consider pulling the plug on the part time job.

Sports teach teamwork, personal achievement, development and perseverance. Sports are so important and helpful in growing maturity and character in your students. The need to be disciplined both athletically and academically is something that I champion; however, if you are looking to create the next LeBron James (basketball) or Tom Brady (football) – I have a different mindset than most. If you son or daughter is so gifted that they consistently rise above the rest of the talent on their team or in their sport, so be it. Let it come to them. Invest in it, but only after they have shown you their academic commitment as well. Remember this book is about academic success. If your student can do both – fantastic. I wholeheartedly support you; but if one area is to be sacrificed, I would say to tone down excessive engagement in sports. The student/athlete is a huge topic, trust me I know. I graduated from Syracuse University and know my share of top tier athletes - the best of the best even. It is a tall order to make it to Division I, let alone go to the Pros. Be careful not to try to make your student a "pro" before they finish their studies. Balance is key. My nephews are great examples of this. They are knocking out their studies, and they are equally talented "ballers". In order to do both, it requires A LOT of effort from both the student and the parent(s).

Own Your GPA

Any student that I have ever tutored, mentored or coached knows that I am keenly interested in how students are doing academically. One key barometer of student's academic success is their grade point average or simply put – their GPA. While grades will not tell you the whole story, they will certainly give you a great summary of where the student is excelling, where they are just making it by and most definitely where they are struggling. Parents often tell me that their student's grades don't really reflect their mastery of a given subject matter. There are comments about the teacher grading "too hard" or giving too much homework; there are statements about the students not being good test takers.

The most important thing to start with is the fact that each student owns their respective GPAs, despite how the grade is achieved. Whether rightly earned or improperly given, grades belong to the students. There are many inputs that yield independent assessments which in turn result in final grades. I want to distinguish here between homework, a quiz, a test, a midterm, a paper or a final exam. There are varying degrees of importance for these graded opportunities, and dependent upon the weight of a given activity, your student may want to be more or less concerned with their score on that assignment or assessment. For instance, if the Unit Test is worth 25% of the quarter or semester grade, it is incumbent upon the test taker to do his or her best given that only 75% of the total grade is still available to be impacted after the results of the test. This is why understanding the class syllabus is so important. The syllabus represents the guidebook for your child – even more so as they advance through their academic career. It is critical to review the syllabus and ask any questions of the teacher on the front end, like: *How much is homework/classwork worth versus the papers, reports and group projects?* Remember, you don't want to be that parent that keeps challenging the teacher about why your kid's grade is what it is without recalling that the syllabus would have cleared things up for you in the beginning.

You should discuss the syllabus with the student's teacher or administrator at the beginning of each class year. No matter the age/grade of your student, the most important is to explain to your student the weight or prioritization of particular grades.

I will share a few more thoughts on grades and how we viewed them in our home. My focus during the pre-high school years was on my kids following instructions and understanding key academic concepts – fact families, reading comprehensions, becoming strong writers. I wasn't overly preoccupied with their grades early on unless they got a "C". While this letter grade means "average" to some, my kids knew that it would spark a conversation with me that they did not want to participate in. Once you know your student's ability and their academic approach, there is far less for you to address outside of the elements mentioned in earlier chapters. The GPA is a real thing once your student enters high school (or when they begin taking HS classes for credit). Progress and midterm reports are opportunities to see if the student's GPA reflected where they felt they should be. Remember the philosophy: there should be no surprises for the student or parent. Know your kids. Once our kids began taking Advanced Placement (AP) courses, there were other motivations (honor roll, 4.0 cumulative awards and other merit recognition) to spur them on as it related to GPA. Whatever the catalyst, let the GPA be their thing.

Introduce the concept early knowing that grades become really important, especially when you are performing beneath your potential. Grades can reflect one's level of understanding or one's difficulty with test taking. Either way, get a handle on it early, and then leave it be [Grades will be discussed more in the scholarship chapter].

Standardized Tests

The subject of standardized tests is a very polarizing topic in that every state (to the best of my knowledge) has some form of aptitude test or assessment for students in elementary, middle and high school. These tests are attempts to let the school system (and the public) know how they are preparing (or not preparing) their students. We will not get too heavy into that matter until we get to the college entrance exam section of the book, but it does garner mentioning. Some key considerations to remember are student preparation, expectations and the proper response afterwards.

While students are not "fans" of the dreaded state tests, they will click their heels with joy knowing that there generally isn't any homework during the days leading up to and inclusive of the lengthy test(s). Before addressing our key considerations, let's remember that the purpose of these tests is to assess how well students know the academic material indicative of a given grade level. The majority of the concepts presented should be quite familiar to your student. In the state of Maryland (my home), I know firsthand that performance on some of these tests is directly or indirectly tied to school funding – so, these tests are super important to many folks. Like it or not. With that thought in mind, ask yourselves if anyone would want your child to perform poorly on the test. Hmm. Absolutely not.

With that in mind, how can a student or family prepare for the assessment exams? First, remind your student that they do NOT need to study for these tests. How about that? Take the unnecessary pressure off of them immediately. No practice problems and no flash cards for this one. Whew!!! Hopefully the clinched fists have been released. Woo-sah. Now that the kids are flush again, tell them that they won't have homework or extra chores during standardized test week. What in the world?! You most definitely have their undivided attention now. They are alert and listening, wondering why they cannot take these exams year-long. LOL. Lastly, let them know that you are going to give them Sunday style breakfast (or at least step up from the normal breakfast for these days) each day of the testing. This will provide the requisite fuel for peak mental performance. Now you still have one piece of news they might not agree with you on and that is an earlier than normal bedtime (at least an hour, dependent on age/grade). Rest is critical, so that the brain can function optimally.

Expectations on the test. As a student, you have to be ready for long periods of time sitting still, not being able to talk or move around, and timed testing. Be ready for it and don't be surprised by it. Unless there are special accommodations requested, you will see this format over and over again throughout your academic career. As a parent, you should want to see what your child really knows. Period. End of discussion. The school is generally overly concerned in the preparation for these tests. Maybe the lead grade level teacher will give some preparation material, but understand that there isn't much you can do unless you get a previous version of the test with a "how to answer problems" guide.

In contrast, the Scholastic Aptitude Test (SAT) is used as an entrance exam for college. You will need to study and have significant preparation over an extended period of time. A quick shout out to *Innovative Study Techniques*

(IST) and my colleague and friend, Ms. Riche Holmes, Esq. for her firm that provided test preparation for students (including all three of ours). At some point during junior year, we would have the kids spend approximately 8-12 weeks in IST's SAT/ACT preparation course. The practice tests, drills and homework assignments all pushed the youngsters, so that they would peak at the time of the actual exam. Our approach was to have them take the test one time before engaging Riche's team. This way we would have a benchmark before engaging with the college students that would serve as tutors and class instructors. The results were gratifying for each of them, in that scores in the 1350-1450 range yielded more merit awards [actually 2 of our kids were Merit semifinalists]. You may say, "I don't have additional resources for a class." One of our daughters won an ACT prep course by engaging with Delta Sigma Theta Sorority, Inc. as part of their young girls mentoring program – Delta Gems. The main idea is to look around for the resources while also addressing the need. I recommended other families, and our kids generally had a classmate or two that participated as well.

Media Consumption

13

This next subject will be a bit sticky, but I want you to hang with me for a minute. We live in a technological age. Our kids have a super computer at their fingertips given the advent of the internet and smart phones. Students can seek out the answers to difficult issues and questions merely by invoking the phrases, "Google it!" or "Ask Siri". Gone are the days of heavy research in the library via microfiche, since much of the content has been made accessible via the computer. That being said, it is important to remember that the computer, our televisions (cable), radios and movies have the ability to educate, inform, entertain and rob our young people of the most valuable of commodities - TIME.

As a latch-key child growing up, I walked home from school, checked in with my neighbor, let myself in the house, got a bowl of cereal, and preceded to watch television every day for an hour or so before starting homework. Before cable television, internet & mass video games, there were a few afterschool specials & shows that were meant to draw your attention - almost babysitting you, until you began your homework and waited for your parents to come home from work.

While at the time, I saw no issue with the mass consumption of television; however, as parents, my wife and I made the radical decision that, despite official days off of school (i.e. spring, summer & winter breaks), there would be NO television watching during the school week. The internet would be used for homework/study/research purposes and cellphones could be used to contact classmates for an assignment or project, otherwise the phones were powered off by 8:00pm or 8:30pm nightly. There were no televisions or computers in their bedrooms (laptops for college students were ok). This philosophy was instituted through 12th grade and HS graduation. While we became more lax the older the students got with respect to bedtimes, cellphone usage & computer usage, television viewing during the week was a mainstay, save elections, American Idol tryouts & the annual family viewing of the Roots miniseries.

Our desire as parents was not to be ogres, but we felt that the school week should be devoted to just that, school. There are plenty of other obligations and distractions like after school clubs, events, community and family commitments. We found that there was plenty of time to watch and consume media. The extent to which you can curb, limit, and restrict for your kids, the better. They aren't really missing anything, only short delays in when they consume multi-media.

Our kids will tell you that we took them to many movies, just maybe NOT on the weekend that they opened. It is all about establishing priorities. Remember our first chapter on STRUCTURE, our kids need us as parents and guardians to help set the tone, so that as they develop and mature, they can handle the prioritization themselves. Sometimes the movies served as rewards, other times they were opportunities for the family or the kid's friends to get together and enjoy some fun entertainment. Whatever the case, the point is that we, as parents, can establish what the respective norms are for the family. Once your family knows how much media is too much media, set the limit and maintain the boundary. It will not be met with excitement and celebration if you are scaling down, but trust me, the proof is in the pudding as they say. If your kids are focused on their studies all week, not all the social media feeds and such, you should see marked improvement in their academics as well as in household engagement. Understand that whatever your children are consuming, they will produce more of. If they consume more mind-numbing Twitter & Instagram - that is what will pour out of them. Open their brains to more research, studying & meaningful communication. I promise you will see a decidedly different result from your son or daughter.

And while I am on this point, just because you turn off the television, social media or smart phone, it doesn't mean there aren't other things that could help augment your child's studying/learning such as sports, museums, fairs, field trips, etc. Remember, it is more about seeing everything as a potential learning opportunity.

Celebrate Student Accomplishments

14

"You've got to mark the occasions." When your student hits a milestone in the band or when they finally are able to do a full lap in the pool - mark it. Celebrate it and make sure that your child realizes that this is not a *regular* event. My wife and I made it a habit of going out for Mexican food (On the Border, I believe) with the kids after report cards came out. *Why Mexican* you might ask. It's because that's where we went very early in the process - when kids liked crayons & activity sheets while waiting for food. The place represented our way of saying, "Kudos". Now mind you, we attempted to pay for A's & B's at some point in time also by mimicking what we had seen somewhere else. We abandoned that quickly. We found that our kids didn't need financial motivation, but they did need positive reinforcement. Acknowledgment - it had everything to do with it.

Even as we celebrate birthdays and anniversaries, we need to spend the requisite time and energy recognizing the academic achievements that our kids reach. While honoring a good report card is one thing, it is equally important to praise meeting an important deadline, knocking out those addition and multiplication tables, successfully presenting in front of the class, collaborating on a group project and knocking out that major essay or paper. All of the aforementioned are opportunities to show your student that what they accomplish is important to you and you create an environment of recognition and celebration.

Also, you should not just validate the result of a good or bad grade. That is an altogether separate step. Here, we merely acknowledge that something great has taken place, and we want to stick a pin in it and mark the occasion. Plain and Simple. Don't overthink this, folks. This idea of "Marking the Occasion" is a wonderful phrase my cousin, Kutimack, shared with me many years ago with respect to relationships. He referenced celebrating milestones in our relationships to aid in strengthening them over time. It was such great advice that I even put it in practice in my own marriage. The same way we celebrate first dates and milestone anniversaries, we also need to highlight and recognize our loved ones' accomplishments. It is an area that we only get better at with practice. I had to learn to appreciate my wife in the day-to-day areas: awesome dinner, love how you explained that lesson to your students [she is an educator], and even cheering ourselves on when we navigated a difficult hurdle – say a debt or disagreement. All were important enough to mark the occasion and pat ourselves on the back. But seriously, it goes to reason, that if our children get consistent, positive feedback and encouragement they begin to internalize the positive reinforcement. They should know that we are their crusaders, cheerleaders and hype-(wo)men. They should not have to look any further than us for this all-too-important support. How much time should it take? Hear me - I did not say buy a gift or go to the mall for shopping (although good options for rewards). You should be creative and deliberate.

Those milestones of recognition become building blocks to the student's academic confidence. Every "great job", "Atta boy" or "Atta girl", "I knew you could do it", creates self-confidence and makes deposits of value and purpose in our youngsters. They will need to tap into this reserve later in their academic and professional careers.

Trust me. For some of us this may be difficult because we did not get the praise and accolades as youngsters, so we believe in more of the same tough love we experienced as kids. I was there too until I realized that our children needed more from me in this arena. If you haven't done this lately, feel free to start right now.

Now you might say, *my kid's grades are low, or their behavior is not worth rewarding.* I would say modify the bar/threshold for your student. Help them establish some goals or objectives as a target for achievement. Make the goals S.M.A.R.T. – Specific. Measurable. Achievable. Realistic. Time-bound. This way, they will be able to do it! When they put in the work – cheer them on.

Just like the example of making a special breakfast during testing week - you want the time to be memorable. You should look forward to those moments in parenting when you can celebrate your kids and love on them, so they know what it feels like to get praise and rewarded at home. It goes a long way. Trust me. You know what? They will begin to duplicate the process - if you're lucky - passing on the quality trait. As your children get up and through their teens it will become equally important to share in the decision about WHAT the celebration looks like. Maybe it's having friends over, a mall outing, or whatever. It doesn't really matter so long as *they* value it. If you

Celebrate Student Accomplishments

are the only one feeling good about the celebration, then it is time to retool and recalibrate.

Not too long ago when I saw that the iPhone cascaded balloons down when you text "CONGRATULATIONS", I was like, "That's what I am looking for" - a chance to send it to someone as an acknowledgement. Finish a tough assignment - send a "Congratulations". Help a classmate when you didn't have to – send a "Congratulations". Turn in a paper early. All worth celebrations. Remember parents - you are attempting to establish norms for your kids. If you celebrate accomplishments, so will they. You are building in them the capacity to be appreciated and to appreciate others. Remember to "Mark the moments."

Graduation Party

While I do not advocate going bananas crazy at a high school graduation (ala Barry Sanders, act like you've been there before), a must have is the graduation celebration. Remember to mark the moments and celebrate achievements. Let your student plan elements of the function, remembering to invite key family, friends, neighbors, mentors and the like. It is an awesome opportunity to allow people to love on your child, especially for those individuals that could not participate in the graduation ceremony itself (given the lack of tickets nowadays). It does take a village and this celebration can recognize the student while simultaneously allowing the graduate to give individual and collective thanks to all of those

Graduation Party

members of his/her village.

The size and scope of your function is entirely up to your budget, space, time and interest. For our family, it was a great opportunity to have a mini family reunion, cookout and have people reconnect. It is great to see generations all together for the purpose of encouraging the graduate while they in turn get to spend one on one time visiting with each of the guests. Now don't get it wrong, this is a full day of work – prep work, engagement during the event, and the crazy cleanup. Even with such a daunting activity, the reward, in my opinion is tremendous. As a parent, I enjoyed seeing everyone having a nice time – seeing my daughters (at their respective graduation celebrations) sharing what their plans were for the future and allowing the graduate to articulate appreciation in their own way (remarks, music play list, thank you notes, etc). We found that this occasion allowed a sense of self-expression for the teenager as well as an opportunity for the greater community to financially launch the honoree into their destiny.

A financial launch. Yes, I said it. Don't look at me crossed-eyed because I mentioned finances, money, gifts. While I won't go into how to address college costs until much later in the book, this launch is unlike what GoFundMe or KickStarter or Rent Parties attempt to accomplish. Those events really are looking to address a clear and specific idea/issue/need, whereas the notion of the graduation celebration financial launch is merely pushing the student into the next dimension – which is not nearly as clear as what the other funding mechanisms are designed for. The student could be going to college and the monies will establish a textbook fund, a travel account to get back and forth home during school breaks, or a clothing allowance to build the wardrobe that will meet the climate of the new campus setting. For the student that will be taking a year to volunteer or join the Peace Corps, the funds will augment their living stipend, or it might be the down-payment for the first "bucket" vehicle that allows them to begin working their first adult job. Whatever the case, the community/neighborhood/church family has the ability to help set the foundation.

Isn't this how it should be? I believe so. *Why*, you may ask. I have watched some of my Jewish and African friends/colleagues and their bar/bat mitzvahs and other ceremonies for kids who are coming of age. These young people, by reason of their age and completing an approved set of classes/studies are ready to go into young man/womanhood. A ceremony is established for them to show what they have learned and to celebrate this milestone in life

Graduation Party

(sound familiar). There is a major celebration held and people sow into the child's life at this particular stage. Not because the child has some fantastic invention or great future plans, but it gives everyone a chance to celebrate and then financially launch them into their future. If we all could adopt this philosophy, I feel we all could be a bit further along. The principle of sowing into others is biblical and morally responsible. "Give and it shall be given unto you, good measure, pressed down, shaken together and running over" (Luke 6:38 NKJV). Now hear me, I am absolutely talking about the student being blessed with cash, checks, gift cards, and the like, but if that cannot happen – allow people to do what they can. It might be providing the student with a phone card or prepaid cell. It might be giving the student a book of stamps and some envelopes to write home. It might be sharing some frequent flier miles for a trip home or a possible study abroad opportunity. Whatever it is, remember the aim/goal is to participate in "launching" them. Webster says the word launch means "to release, catapult, or sendoff; to give (a person) a start; to put into operation or set in motion". I love these definitions. The post high school diploma phase will require a new level of support and launching. Parents can and should play an important part at this pivotal juncture for our young people. I hope so. Loosen your purse strings and take the vice grip off the wallet because there will be more discussions about the cash, the dollars, the money, el dinero throughout this book. Smile. It is all good. As Bishop T.D. Jakes asks, "Can we go deeper?" Let's do it.

Majors and Minors

We are now into the section of the book that most folks believe is very important. I would add a caveat here that you need to really have the input/engagement of your college-bound student AND a good working knowledge of them, as an individual.

Some might be asking why are we discussing this at the onset of chatting about paying for college; I would suggest to you that one›s intended course of study could have significant bearing on the kind and amount of money vis à vis scholarships, grants and fellowships that could be available for your student. Please know that your student is ultimately responsible for the path that he or she chooses, academically; but I feel it is the parent's/guardian's/mentor's role to supply the student with adequate intel [military term use for inside info or intelligence], so they can make an informed decision about which way to proceed academically.

When it was mentioned earlier about knowing your student in high school, it was no joke. Understanding not only their likes, but also their dislikes is key to developing a narrower focus for college. Please hear me on this. Your student may not know exactly which aspect of engineering they want to study right now, but it is important to know if they have any affinity to advance on an engineering track. If your child has been harping on religion and philosophy, then be sure to marry the discussion up with salary estimates for the profession and what a liberal arts curriculum might look like.

One of our daughters took it upon herself to look into personality tests and such to see what type of fields were more closely aligned to her interests and passion areas - socially, societally, and personally. It wasn't so much that these tests or assessments dictated her decision, but what they did was allow her to look into some parallel and tangential study areas that she might not have ordinarily considered. Here I want to put a plug in for doing your research. This does not only apply to scientists and professors, but for us all. If we want to make more informed decisions, it will require advanced research. Back to our example of a possible engineering major, additional questions that could help might revolve around:

- What type of areas could a student with this major find work?
- Does one need an advanced degree beyond what is taken during undergraduate studies?
- How many years will it take to complete this degree?

Seeking out the answers to these and other questions can give your student more background to determine which path to pursue academically.

Now you are probably still asking yourself, *what is the corollary between major and financial assistance for college.* There are majors attached to disciplines that have a higher priority nationally/internationally, thus there are significantly more dollars available from institutions of higher education and those industries seeking to hire individuals that matriculate/graduate from said colleges/universities. Case in point – Science, Technology, Engineering and Math (STEM) is among one of our nation's highest educational priorities given our low ranking worldwide [38 out of 71 in Math, 24 out of 71 in Science (Pew Research)]. This can translate into effectively more scholarships, internships and opportunities IF your student has an affinity for any of the related STEM fields.

On the other hand, there may not be a lot of funding for nursing majors (health services fields) in college, but significant financial assistance for the requisite nursing programs post-undergraduate studies. It just depends. My aim is to make you aware of what you are facing. Another example is one regarding quite popular majors such as business, liberal arts and psychology. Know that these majors are broad and generic and thus many students will pour into these programs of study. Here you will potentially find over saturation and little to no specific scholarships. If found, there are considerably more folks applying and the likelihood of award shrink. Please remember that I am starting the discussion on funding college by asking each of you to evaluate what you might study, first, so that where you go next points you in a particular direction of funding that matches/aligns with your student's desired path. Don't take what I have shared as a reason not to major in the non-STEM areas - on the contrary. As *School House Rock!* taught me, "Knowledge is power". There may be corporate scholarships available for these majors, but again, I want you to do your homework and research. As a parent know this: your student's major/minor or the combination thereof might change. I know from firsthand experience. You will feel some kind of way;

but again, this degree will be theirs in the end. What they do with it will be their life's work. The teachers, coaches, mentors and those networks that you put around them can help influence and inform their decision making.

College Tours vs. College Visits

How will your student know where they want to attend if they have not visited the campus? Many folks are making one hundred-thousand-dollar decisions without having set foot in a building, classroom, dormitory or neighboring vicinity. I want to chat with you about how you can remedy that.

I see college visits and tours as two entirely different things. Let's look at each one and see how they are both of help to a family while fulfilling individual goals. College tours can be done formally or informally. You literally can drive to most campuses, park your vehicle in a space and begin walking around the grounds. This is how we began to introduce college to our kids. When we went out of

College Tours vs. College Visits

town to visit family or take a mini vacation, we could stop by any college in route and make a stop. We would look at the architecture and layout of the buildings, check out the facilities (the ones that were open and public), have lunch in a cafeteria, see what was going on in the bookstore, peruse the community plaza or strip mall to see how the town and college interact. In my opinion, all of this can be done on an informal tour. A formal tour, on the other hand, might include a student guide who can share particular tidbits about the university, some facts regarding the campus and student life. This can be quite informative if your tour guide is good and well versed on the school. You can ask some questions, so long as the student representative knows and is willing to answer. Remember that the tour is just that - a tour. It will not be a visit to all the buildings or facilities. It will be finite in terms of how long. Most times, dormitories are not included because of privacy concerns and dependent on the tour group size, it might be overly quick.

If the tour is your only option, please do your homework (advanced reading) before arriving on campus. This way you can make the most of your tour. Many schools have virtual tours on their websites (high tech at its best, for sure). While this will be a very nice and scripted view of the campus, it will not replace the real thing. You will not get a real sense of the terrain, the distance between buildings, the incline that will impact things when there is inclement weather (ala my time at Syracuse University in the snow). Always consider that you want to have the most information possible when deciding where your student will ultimately go to school. The college tour is a great tool to get informed.

In my humble opinion, the college visit is a step further in your knowledge gathering exercise. Where the tour stops, the visit goes into more specifics about the university, programs/majors, student life, clubs and the like. It is less about where things are but how things are. Some schools have an information session during the college visit. This is a time when merit (scholastic) or need based financial aid are discussed by representatives in Finance and Admissions. Students cannot give you the nitty gritty as it pertains to what the school is looking for in terms of the next incoming class of freshmen.

College visits afford you the opportunity to hear from faculty and students that are part of your intended major/program of study so make sure it includes an information session or meeting that allows for a presentation by a school representative and subsequent question and answer period. Here you can probe about all the matters that concern you. Additionally, you can be candid with respect to the financials. What is this school's position on financial aid? Is it all need based or is there some merit based as well? Here you get to drill down to the questions that really matter to you and ask them of those who really have the answers. For example, if your student wants to study abroad, you ask if that can be done and still allow for graduation in 4 years. These sessions are sometimes 90 minutes or longer depending on the agenda. Sometimes they are offered on the same day as a college tour, but often are separate. By engaging with staff, you can connect with individuals who can assist before, during and after the admissions process. You can harken back to your visit and rekindle the connection from there. These visits are tracked by the school and you want them to know you are interested – well before you apply. Any chance you get to travel as a family, look to tack an impromptu college visit on the front or back end. Even if the school in the area is not on your student's radar. Campus visits can spark discussion and inquiry. At worst, you might get an "I don't like this" or "I don't like that". It would be easy to peek into the dining hall, check on the proximity to public transportation, and find out whether or not amateur sports are available all while in town for this visit. Other things to consider include taking off on alternating Mondays, Thursdays, piggy-back on 2-hour early dismissal days from school and get on the road early; coordinating with some other parents and make it a group thing to optimize costs and driving duties, and taking in a game or activity while on campus.

Another key difference in how you explore colleges is knowing the purpose of the college trip. What do you want as an intended outcome? During our middle school and early high school years, we wanted to expose, inspire and make our students aware of colleges. Taking them to events at local schools and subsequently getting them more comfortable with the "feel" of college was the objective. Eventually, we wanted to shift focus and make our college visits more strategic. These trips should help you to better assess the institution and allow you to rate/rank it in relation to the other schools being considered. Sometimes I would just plan an impromptu visit while we were traveling somewhere else. Other times, it was a deliberate trip to see one or more campuses. Whatever the rationale – make it happen. Some of our visits caused us to remove a university from the list or to confirm what the marketing information conveyed.

In a nutshell, take advantage of the sundry ways to see and visit your list of schools. Whether it be a virtual tour, informal or formal onsite tour or an actual college visit - make sure that you are fully versed in what that college has to offer - on and off the brochure. Some things you will need to see for yourself. Things like proximity to religious places of worship or off-campus recreation, malls, etc. will all require an in-person visit. See it as an opportunity to bond with your student or even invite some of your child's friends and parents. I often volunteered to drive and another parent handled gas or tolls. You can do a day trip or overnighter. Some entities do college tours that last from a few days to approximately a week. Figure out what you ultimately want to accomplish and decide which type of visit is most appropriate. Good luck!

18

Selecting Your School

I want to take a slightly unorthodox approach with respect to this area given your student is now ready to decide on a college. Similar to choosing the right major, it is doubly important to select the right college or university to complete your undergraduate degree. As there are a multiplicity of majors/minors to choose from, there are literally thousands of colleges to choose from. Your family's ability to narrow that search will be instrumental in your student's academic/life success as well as potentially driving some of the financial decisions that will follow in the upcoming chapters. Because the focus of this section of the book is financial, I will not give an exhaustive lesson on selecting a college, but I will touch on enough for you to get well informed on the key elements.

Here are some key factors: Will you attend a state or private school? Will it be rural or urban? What will the size be (in terms of overall student body and expanse of the campus)? Where is the college/university located and how might the student get back and forth? Is the course of study a strong program element at this given institution? Does the school have the extracurricular opportunities for students that address needs/wants identified by your student? To me, all of these come BEFORE how much does it cost. If the school cannot or does not, with a certain level of proficiency address the above, then why is said school even in the discussion? As you will see, cost is important, but for my family we chose to lower it as a priority on the school choice list.

Once you have identified a reasonable number of colleges that fit your student's "profile", you should begin schedule college visits for the top 5-7, if you cannot visit them all. Note: I would keep your initial scope to no more than 15 schools. Remember, there are thousands to choose from [ideally identify 10-20 of interest], so you will have to research and make some assumptions.

College Affordability

Oh no, he didn't tell me to look at colleges for my child on the basis of cost! That could be what you are feeling right now. Honestly, if someone told me the same thing, absent the knowledge I have, I might well have the exact same sentiment. Hang with me, I am going somewhere with this.

What you did not hear me say is that you should compromise the rigor of the academic programming. You did not hear me say to find the cheapest school. I suggest that you look for schools that you can afford without aid. "There are over 4200 degree-granting postsecondary institutions in the United States" [US News & World Report, 2/15/2019, *"A Guide to the Changing Number of*

U.S. Universities"]. Let that sink it for a minute. Of all these schools, you very well might find several that your household could include in your budget.

Now, you will have to do your research, and you will have to do your homework to figure out what your household can reasonably fit into the budget. If you do not know about budgets/money, check out a few of my go to resources in Chapter 21-Saving. Remember when I mentioned earlier that there would need to open and honest communication, well here we are! As a parent or guardian, you don't want to have a discussion on what you can and cannot afford after your student has begun applying to all the Ivy League and $60K per year schools. Be a part of the process. Understand that I am only talking about the true cost of the institution at this point and time. We will address financial aid, scholarships, grants, and the like soon enough.

We have to set realistic expectations from the outset as to what can be afforded in order to attend college without the burden of debt to the student or the family. Your family free application for federal student aid (FAFSA) score will drive what most colleges consider as your expected family contribution (EFC) - also known as what you *should* be able to spend. It doesn't matter whether you agree or not, this is the basis that financial aid packages are built upon.

Because this aid is not finalized until the late spring of your student's senior year of high school, it is critically important to already know your figures. This will help to narrow the choices/options, and it can give you a stronger place from which to negotiate, if possible.

Now in subsequent chapters we will discuss various savings vehicles that are intended to help defray what you will need to absorb from your household budget. All of this information needs to be considered when your family addresses the cost of college. Another comment that arises when talking about affordability is that your child will get scholarships, so you can look at any school you want. That is a great comment, especially if your student knocked out the first part of this book regarding academic success. If so, there *may* be scholarships available, but then the real question is: how much scholarship money is available given my student's academic success? Is it $5K annually? Is it 50% tuition? Maybe even a full ride. The only way you will know is to get ahead of the curve. Get the answers to these questions *before* you need to know.

Here are some tips. Ask the school's financial aid representative the following questions:

- What are the ranges of merit awards (aka scholarships)?

College Affordability

- What are the associated GPA & SAT scores necessary to achieve the highest amount of scholarship award?
- What cumulative GPA is required to maintain these awards?

These answers coupled with your school cost and FAFSA intel should help paint a clearer picture of the net cost for attending the various schools. Make sure to factor the following often omitted costs/expenses:

- attire based on the climate/weather of given school,
- transportation to & from school,
- money for extra-curricular activities/clubs/sports,
- personal expenses,
- computer/printing needs, and
- miscellaneous

Now you should have enough information to make an informed decision about which colleges are in the categories that I rate: comfortable, within reach or way outta' reach. These categories are good for financial and overall academic assessment. The comfortable category is just that - comfortable. Your academic merit would be adequate to get you in the school and the corresponding costs reflect the same. All the way around, this is doable. Nothing wrong with having 2-3 of the schools on your list fitting this category. The school(s) in the reach category means that it will require some added effort - you will have to push yourself on the standardized tests, max out the GPA and write really strong essays for admissions package. These are not extraordinary feats, but for some students this will be a stretch for the parents to afford. These schools may accept the student, but absent the highest academic marks, there will be little to no merit awards commensurate with the higher costs of these reach schools. Be aware. Lastly there are the schools in the way outta' reach category. These could be your upper tier state universities (i.e. Cal Tech, UNC-Chapel Hill, or UMD-College Park) or your Ivy League institutions (i.e. Stanford, Princeton, or Brown). In either case, these are the most selective universities in the country and they cost the most (caveat: they also have some of the largest endowments, so admission generally comes with a significant financial package). Again, know the college and what their endowment could do for an admitted student.

I digress. Some of the ideas above also speak directly to how you should select your college - remember all of these fact-finding missions are to aid your family in making the best decision. I am merely addressing the fiscal side of the decision.

Scholarships

As the saying goes, "you got to play to win". Scholarship searches should begin in 8th - 9th grade. Students should fill out applications before they are due and get familiar with processes. It is NEVER too early to start seeking out financial resources to support, cover or augment the funds needed to pay for higher education. The sooner you begin this process, hopefully the more fluid and less arduous it will become for your family.

The reason I say to start in middle school is so that your student can get familiar with their own writing style which is vital to handling all of the assorted essay prompts (topics & subjects). Students need to have a healthy sense of who they are and what they think regarding a vast number of things. We will talk more about the nature of scholarships, but you must understand that at the core of scholarship applications is completion, great writing & volume. Students have to figure out which applications they qualify for, so that they are not wasting time. Time is a commodity, and it is precious; therefore, I highly recommend using some sort of calendaring system to keep track of the applications and their associated due dates.

While we are here let›s discuss this very administrative part of the scholarship process. In order to get to the money, you have to recognize that things are done in an orderly fashion and should be addressed as such. No haphazard approach to scholarships will return what you want for your student. There have to be deliberate actions, at specific times, so you can achieve your goals. Up front, I must tell you that there aren't any guarantees.

There are a myriad of types/categories of scholarships. Some are focused on community involvement, where the impetus of the resulting scholarship is related to the impact on a community effort or goal. Many, if not most, are merit based - meaning they are predicated on your student's grades or scholastic aptitude. In addition, there will be large swaths of scholarships that are decided by the income of your household. Be mindful to look at your local school and congressional districts. Find opportunities that are civic focused, minority based (if applicable), or based on academic discipline. Note that this is

NOT an exhaustive list. Remember this effort will require work. You can also use resources such as: United Negro College Fund (UNCF), Fastweb, The College Board or apps like Scholly.

Let's go deeper. You have to figure out whether it is advantageous to apply for a given scholarship. I know you believe that your child will get that Coca Cola award, but I just want you to be aware that there are approximately 100K other students thinking the same thing, then it is narrowed down to about 2,000 semifinalists and 150+ awardees. Hear me, I am not saying to eliminate certain scholarships, but I do want you to be realistic as you plan where to apply. This leads me to the notion of strategy. *How does one address scholarship applications in a strategic manner?* One way is to create some basic thematic essays. Another way to think about it is to consider creating focused essays: biographical (self-focused), volunteer (outward focused), or academic (major or education focused), you get the point. While the essay prompts may change, having a few, core paragraphs on the above can go a long way in cutting down the time needed to complete your applications.

Another way to be more strategic is to find out the requirements and begin gathering the necessary documents well before they are due. This means parents having their most recent tax returns so that they can be easily accessed since some scholarships are income based. After a while you will get more savvy as to which ones your family will NOT qualify for based on too much income. Don't get hung up on whether or not you believe the criteria. If the application is targeting only Pell Grant eligible students, then your income generally cannot exceed $60,000. You can be eligible to receive one to help you pay for college if your EFC is significantly less than your cost of attendance (COA). No need to waste time completing an application and writing an essay for a scholarship the student should not have begun. You are wasting time. Stop it. Need based is just that. Throughout this book I have shared the importance of students learning and becoming more comfortable with writing. This is primetime for those skills to shine. My kids – all three of them – had to participate in this process of obtaining scholarships. They wrote essays to sororities and fraternities, their local church, auxiliaries, corporations, and the universities themselves. For our family, scholarships accounted for approximately 60% of the total cost of attending the kid's schools. With costs (tuition, room and board and other fees) from freshman year to graduation totaling more than $160K (low end) and close to $300K (high end), sixty percent is no amount to sneeze at. Let me say this while here, there were several schools that offered full rides (100% costs covered), others had packages that were approaching 70-80% coverage but they were offered at schools that ranked a bit lower than our final choice. Remember, we were interested in options. These scholarships – no matter where they were from – offered our family the opportunity to have further discussions about what we ultimately wanted to do.

Equally, your student should have created their academic resume and kept it updated, so that it can be quickly uploaded upon demand. Students should also be prepared to get a stack of transcript request forms from their Guidance Office at the high school (or University) depending on the type of scholarship. Most will have a minimum GPA requirement. Adhere to it. If they ask for 3.6 cumulative GPA, you sending in an application with a 3.3 is a waste of time. Stop it. This section is about being strategic – doing things that put your students in a place for greater successful outcomes. As discussed earlier in the book, senior year is already filled with enough challenging elements, and this facet, while critically important, is an add-on. This means that the time commitment necessary is above and beyond all the academic, athletic, extracurricular and family obligations. Strategic aides will be vital for your student's ability to cope with all that is being asked of them. It goes without saying that time management is one of your greatest allies. When you have time to get something started or completed, do it. More often than not, "free time" will be in short quantity.

Save Early & Often

Save early and often using various plans such as: 529, Coverdale, state college prepaid plans... do something! This chapter will hurt you to the core because WE – parents, guardians, and adults represent the greatest deterrent for addressing savings. I should have actually renamed this section: <u>SAVE period</u>. Nothing else should be written because SAVE period is reiterating the principal point. We must have the concept of saving ingrained in our person, or it will be futile to dialogue further. If you saved for your first car, follow those steps. If you saved for prom, repeat the process. If by chance you saved for the down payment on your house or a dream vacation, I am asking you to harken back to what sacrifices you needed to make to reach the desired goal, BUT this time do it for someone else – your child. I told you it would be rough.

I am the child of parents where one parent went to college and the other went on to serve in the Air Force and later Vietnam. They didn't save for college as the concept of $20K per year (circa 1990) for private college/university was far different than the $2500 at Hampton Institute (1965). They taught me saving, but borrowing was for houses and it would have to be good enough for paying college costs also. My dad saved money. He never spent much on himself; constantly reminding me that you should not spend all you have. You MUST save for another day. He said that when he received some of his early career paychecks, he would take some "off the top" and set it aside. If the check was for $221.45, he would take the $21.45 and put in a jar or case and then only use the remaining $200. What discipline! He replicated that process over a lifetime. Why do I interject this story here? What does this have to do with saving for college? While my parents didn't save for my college, they assisted me with the student loan payments [they paid a few years, and I have the remaining balances]. They vowed for better in the next generation. They helped save towards supporting their grandkids going to college. Their diligence in taking care of their finances resulted in an ability to gift their grandkids with significant dollars upon graduation from high school. What gift will you impart to the next generation of your family? What will you sow into their academic futures? You will need to examine your own family to determine it, but sit with that story a little bit and reflect as you read more on college saving. They didn't gift bikes, cars, apartments or excessive clothes. They gave a gift that could keep on giving...long past the gift date.

The aim in saving for college is to afford you and your student with options. Maybe it comes down to only one option for school, but with some savings, at least you do have an option for college as opposed to no school at all. Some of your students will not get offered a scholarship, fellowship, grant or financial award (other than a loan). Let me be the first to tell you that this is a sobering thought. I tell you that, not to be rude, but so that you know what you are up against. If you don't save, research, study and follow the guidance of this book (and others of the same elk), you could find yourself in a place where it is your job (or your student's) to fund college. While difficult – it can still be done. Maybe it will take longer than average to finish your degree. That is still ok because it doesn't matter how fast you finish, but that you do indeed finish. If there aren't any additional monies and your student is still inclined to go to college, you will have to look at having them work through college. As financial advisor and creator of *7 Baby Steps*, Dave Ramsey suggests sometimes you have to take "baby steps" to reach your financial goals.

No matter what season you are in life, it is a good time to start saving. If you are planning to have a baby, start a savings account for the baby. If you already had the baby, start a college savings plan. Once your baby is born, go to the bank or online and start a bank account and a 529 plan (more later in this chapter). Even if your child is in high school, like my daughter was, begin to do something – <u>intentionally</u>. That is honorable and speaks to someone else's needs as more important than your own. In order to save you have to know what you have available and know that you need to budget. I won't go into those details here, but I would recommend you to a great resource, Michelle Singletary – Washington Post personal, finance columnist and author of *The 21 Day Financial Fast*. Her financial fast is legendary, and it can help you set your financial house in order. Dave Ramsey can then walk you through the *7 Baby Steps* and *Financial Peace.*

Back to the message – start at what is comfortable but DO SOMETHING. I challenge you to look at the Starbucks latte, the Domino's pizza receipt, the Powerball tickets that line your waste basket and the assortment of shoes, golf attire/clubs, etc. and find some amount that you can save immediately. Try to save $5, $25, or $50 per month and build from there. Systematic and consistent savings will create a nest egg that can grow and develop until the time is right for harvest.

I have mentioned savings accounts, but I want to introduce you to a financial instrument called a 529 plan. In a nutshell, they were designed to help families save for college costs. For example, in Maryland, information can be found at https://maryland529.com. Placing funds in these accounts not only allow your savings to grow with some interest like banks, but you can write off certain amounts based on your state of residency. There are a variety of college savings vehicles such as Coverdell education savings accounts, investment plans, bonds and the like. It doesn›t matter what vehicle or method you use initially. What does matter is that you (repeat after me) - DO SOMETHING. Some of my friends fully funded their kid's 529 plan, others haven't started and many are in the middle – living life. Do I wish I saved more earlier? Yes, but that didn't stop me from trying to increase our savings more and more each year.

Savings via this methodology grows similar to your retirement and investment accounts by compounding interest. The longer the time to save, the greater the potential growth of the investment. Remember any money saved towards college costs reduces the amount needed when tuition bills come due.

Large car notes and expensive vacations will no doubt pull resources away from your savings goals, but these are parent's decisions. Your call. Choose to give them a hype prom and senior trip to name-your-location, or give them the gift of college education that doesn't strap them or you with debt.

Paying for College

I want to stay with the theme of how you can afford the rising cost of college without taking loans. For those of you who might get sleepy in the eyes when people discuss money, finances and the like, I am going to ask that you get your coffee or Red Bull now because I need you wide awake. In an effort to stay ahead of the game, I want to remind you that scholarships are a key way that college costs can be mitigated. I talked about it at length in the scholarship chapter but I wish to remind you that it is merely one of several viable options to paying for college. The early bird gets the worm is an adage that speaks to preparation, readiness and proper prioritization. In order to get the worm – its sustenance – the bird had to set some other things in motion before it could reap the reward. We have to do the same thing with respect to paying for college.

Let's start with a very basic approach using our savings and certificates of deposit (CDs). These are easy to locate at your bank or credit union. Most will allow for low entry amounts such as $250 or $500 to start the accounts, while others have provisions for automatic direct deposit with as low as $25 per month. You might be saying that college costs are more than $25, and I would agree with you wholeheartedly; yet I would submit to you that colleges and universities accept all dollars. The aim is to begin somewhere so that you can set a strategy for tackling the entire bill. The early bird reminds us not to procrastinate. When you read this, think about what day this week will you start your CD, if you don't already have one.

You may also want to designate what a given CD might be earmarked for: the housing deposit, textbooks, a semester of a meal plan, etc. You decide. Establish a SMART (Specific, Measurable, Achievable, Realistic and Time Sensitive) goal and start working towards it. I promise you that the moment you begin saving, your goal will become more and more attainable by the month/year. Often our biggest fear is the unknown or the hugeness of the task ahead of us. In order to move forward, you need to chunk the big stuff down to manageable portions. It applies to studying, savings and reaching goals.

Another great feature of the CD is its liquidity. That means its ability to be converted to cash. This process is relatively easy, but you will need to review the terms of the specific CD. The length of time for maturity will drive the interest to be earned and clue you in on penalties for early withdrawal. My intent is not to give you a financial lesson, suffice it to say your bank or financial advisor will give you all the details, but you won't be wholly in the dark when talking with them.

Another tried and true method of paying for college is plain old work. Apply for a job, show up for X number of hours weekly, do the assigned task(s) and collect a paycheck. This may sound foreign in the midst of sharing on scholarships and CDs, but the principle is a great one. Honest work will yield results that can be deposited and/or invested for future gain(s). This kind of work can occur during breaks from school – winter, spring or summer. The resulting funds can then be applied to the creation of CDs, student bank accounts for travel and incidentals; etc. Remember the aim is to create options. The more options you have, conceivably the better choices/selection scenarios you have.

This concept extends to the financial aid known as Federal Work Study (FWS) program for those students who qualify for it. If your student qualifies, your college can pay the student for jobs that are funded by federal dollars. While many students spend this money on sundry items, the true intent is to offset the cost of college. That is the primary purpose. Don't forget.

If you cannot get a work study job, get a non-work study one. *What does that look like?* you may ask. It looks like a regular job like working in the dining hall, cafe, school store, gymnasium, etc. Be deliberate, especially if this is a needed funding source.

A payment plan is another way to aid families in budgeting for college costs on a month-to-month basis. Say for instance that the semester expenses total $5,000. You may not have the full $5,000 available on the due date, so many universities offer a 3-, 4- or 6-month payment plan. This plan usually can be set up with a low administrative fee and no interest. The family could build these college plan costs into their monthly household budget. This is a "pay as you go" plan. By doing this you do not incur loans, and you consistently pay down what you own to the university/college. This is another often unused option. By going this route our family paid for college expenses – debt free. I will share more our specific approach later in the book, but know that the payment plan – for us – was vital.

Consider the Investment in Your Student

Treat your student's college experience as an investment. While they continue to find themselves academically, emotionally and personally, parents and guardians will be subject to the often vacillating and whimsical nature with which they approach school, classes, major/minor selection, etc. In order to properly assess what the parental engagement should be, financially, one must know their student and figure out how to monetize the pending collegiate experience. Every day we make financial decisions when we eat out for lunch, whether or not we go to the movies or watch FX to see the 15th running of *Shawshank Redemption*. All of these opportunities allow us, delicately or forcibly, to make decisions on how we invest our time and money and to what degree. My recommendation is that you, as the primary investor in your student's academic career, assess the viability of the proposed investment. Simply put: you need to treat their collegiate experience as an investment. Should you view it as the next great Uber, Apple or AirBnB, or should you tread cautiously and not go with the "true daily double" – wagering all that you have when you really don't know much about 16th century inventors. Are you following me? Let me see if I can explain further.

If you are not sure about how to gauge your son or daughter's college success potential, you need only look back to recent history as a sign of future performance. What did high school tell you about them? If you just had a gag reflex, don't worry, it's okay because sometimes there are outliers. This means that your student may have had a difficult high school phase and they are now ready for primetime. You will be one of the strongest witnesses in what you observed over the previous four years. Did you see growth and progress? Did they mature and develop during their matriculation through high school? How did they handle adversity and difficulty? When working alone or in group dynamics, what did you see? It may seem like I am peppering you with a lot of questions, but how else will

Consider the Investment in Your Student

you will how much to invest. Maybe you are thinking that I am too harsh. Somehow that we should invest equally in our children and give each of them a fighter's chance. I beg to differ. As we addressed early in this book, some field/career choices I would not advocate for the students to go to college. If that is true, then why shouldn't we apply a similar litmus test when evaluating college readiness? If your recollection of your student's study habits (or the lack thereof), test preparation (or the absence of this skill), procrastination and being ill prepared versus being proactive and organized is not a rosy memory, you may need to have another conversation with yourself and your student.

Am I saying not to invest in your student, absolutely not! What I am saying is to really look deeper into whether or not paying $40K+ per year is the BEST investment if a 70-80% average is what you have been accustomed to seeing. In like manner, was there steady, positive development as sophomore year turned to junior then senior year? If the proverbial trend line is heading in an upward direction, then the future investment might be well worth it. Consider this: when you buy a used car from the dealership, you are deciding how much is too much to pay for it based on the mileage, wear and tear, remaining warranty (if any), and any associated bells and whistles. After factoring all of these things you decide if the price is right for a purchase. You might get a CarFax report to ensure that there are no hidden accidents and deficiencies; suffice it to say, you do your homework. I am merely asking you to do the same thing here. We want to set our children up for success, right? Then, let's be helpful in fostering a dialogue of realistic expectations. Conversations of community college prior to attending a 4-year college or university would be appropriate at this time. Remember we are talking about value propositions. There will have to be serious talks over multiple sessions/engagements to glean the answers to many of these underlying questions. Understand this. You cannot figure this out August 1st of the year when your student leaves for freshman orientation, but unfortunately, this is when many families begin to have these crucial confabs. While it is great to have them at any time; the sooner, the better.

For those of you who have ever signed up for your 401K or 403B retirement plans, you generally receive a prospectus in the mail to inform you about the mutual fund or stock that you are preparing to buy. Most of us glance over this important information because it can be boring, confusing and lengthy to read. Families need to go through the process of reviewing prospectus data on our students - pull up the report card, solicit teacher feedback, ask for a few writing samples (especially if you have not reviewed much of their junior/senior year essay and English assignments). Standardized tests and subject tests give you much of the data that you will need to make your investment. Investing is not for the faint of heart. For many it might be just as easy to say, "Go to school wherever you want", or "I was only responsible to get you through high school, it's on you now." Either way, burying your head in the sand does not make the wisest of investment strategies. Try this: ask for a trustworthy friend, colleague or family member to give an objective opinion or feedback. Be prepared for what you hear. You are looking for someone that knows you (and hopefully your student), and they can provide vital input. Think about it this way – if when looking back over the body of work called high school, do the actions and options elicit more or less confidence in your student.

Our Family Strategy for No Student Loans

I mentioned earlier that I would share the quintessential element of what our family did to address the tuition costs for two students attending college at the same time. This method was also utilized as our youngest attended an even more expensive university than his older sisters. Here is the chief strategy that we employed:

With my wife and I having three children, and two of them being within 17 months of each other, having two incomes was essentially a "no brainer". When the girls were younger my wife stayed home to raise them for almost 6 years (which included the first 4 years for our son). Because we had accumulated student loan debt and credit cards, it

Our Family Strategy for No Student Loans

was tough back then to live on one income. There were no extra trips, no fancy, newer rides, and the used townhouse had to wait after living with my parents for two years. During that season of our lives, it seemed impossible to save for college; heck, we were knee deep in diapers, formula and month to month survival. My wife began to stay home with our girls after assessing what daycare was doing to our budget and the fact that we wanted the kids to have more "home raising" on the front end. I took part time security positions on the nights and weekends to try to keep us at a particular level financially until my wife returned to work part-time and then eventually full time. This put us back on track as a two-income household after six years of being an only one-income household.

Each story has a lesson – fast forward nine years and our oldest is graduating from high school and preparing to head off to Spelman. We hadn't saved enough, and I am trying to figure out how we will pay for school without borrowing. We had put the other elements of the book into motion (scholarships, payment plans, grants, some savings), but how will we pay the month-to-month obligations, especially when our second daughter would begin college the next year.

Admittedly the panic and anxiety started setting in until I clearly heard in my spirit, "Just live on one income". This was something that my wife's grandmother mentioned to us earlier in our relationship/marriage. Ok, that sounded good, but we were already living on TWO incomes and needed every red cent. We also lived in the Washington, DC area and it took everything to barely get by. I had to reconcile this in my analytical brain for quite a while. I even called a friend who led a one-income household for quite a while. His advice was to strip my household budget down and then do it some more. Upon doing this, I got our budget down to a place where we needed my income and approximately 1/3 - 1/5 of my wife's salary. I felt like we had failed, but remember when I talked about *starting somewhere*, this is the reason why. By the time sophomore year rolled around for our oldest and freshman year for our next student, I was covering our household expenses on my income alone.

We then allocated 100% of my wife's pay to the college account (tuition and room & board). These dedicated funds were always available for withdrawal or payment of the monthly university bill. Was it tight? You bet. But every semester we would "mark the occasion" of having paid off the Fall or Spring costs. No loans. No debt. Now, we didn't buy the kids cars in college, but we covered books, a bi-weekly allowance for incidentals (movies, hair supplies, nice dinner out and of course the blasted Uber

Our Family Strategy for No Student Loans

account, LOL). The kids did not live lavishly, but with each semester, things got easier because we all knew the drill – first payment due in July.

Fast forward a bit further, and our first student is beginning senior year at Spelman. She remained off campus to continue saving some money on housing costs. In July, we know the belt gets tighter and then loosens before the major holidays. "We got this. We have planned for this." Our second daughter lived off campus also while attending Seton Hall University in South Orange New Jersey, and things were definitely more expensive up North. How did we handle the two rental payments in the same month? By having honest communication with the roommate's parent, that's how. Our challenge was cash-flow and the timing of payments due. Expenses were really heavy in July through October. If we could finish paying tuition by mid-October then we could handle paying double rent from November forward. So, that is exactly what we negotiated with the other family. They would cover the first six months of rent, and we would cover the last six months. The end result was that bills were paid and no debt was incurred.

Please hear me, I am NOT saying that we didn't feel our own sense of angst from time to time; we too ask the same questions, "Will we have enough?" "What more will we have to sacrifice?" "When will this season end?" As echoed in the famous Dr. Martin Luther King, Jr. speech – "How long, … Not long". We were a mere five months and approximately $2000 from having paid undergraduate studies off in FULL- zero balance, zero loan. It was a tough road, but with each rent, tuition or other scholarly focused payment, I realized how close we were to our goals as a family.

Students Must be Active in the Process

Sometimes in order to put the correct amount of emphasis on a thing, we state it upfront and then state it again on the back end. That is what I am hoping to do here as I close out this book. I want to reiterate how critically important it is to have your student not only participate in the collegiate process but be an ACTIVE participant. At every twist and turn there is an opportunity for your student to take the lead in their future. Figuring out which way to go with respect to college and how to finance it, requires the engagement of all members of the family – namely your student. As a parent, we at times can try to revisit our youth through our children. While it may seem harmless, it could stunt our kids from much needed development. I have learned firsthand that when I engage my own students, early and often, they begin to understand the subtle nuances of decision making as well as start to find out what they want. The type of classes, majors/minors, school choice, interests and opportunities – all must be considered when making their collegiate decisions.

At the end of the day, whether mom, dad, guardian or other believes it, the collegiate experience has EVERYTHING to do with the student/burgeoning adult. When we discussed earlier the impacts of following certain field of study paths and how they can forecast future earnings (salary), it is necessary to remember that inevitably these decisions are going to be made by 17–21 year-olds. While a scary proposition, I can feel your angst, it is also a necessary one. These young adults are going to make some errors; this is how we all develop and learn. Remember how many times we changed our major, took a random class because two of our friends were taking the same class, thought we wanted to do forensics because it looked cool on the *Criminal Minds* show.

Do we stop coaching our students? No. Do we stop imparting wisdom? Certainly not. *They need us more than ever, yet in a very different way. You may be asking yourself, after following me down this particular path in the book, why should I care so much about what my son or daughter does? They are 18-21 years old and I did my part. I am done. I am not looking to pay for college, not looking to be engaged academically any further. If they want to get all that debt, that is not my problem.* These and many other similar comments express a particular sentiment that can isolate a student and cause them to see themselves on an island of sorts. Trust me, if students think that they are in it alone, they will begin to form ideas apart from your guidance and model; you then wonder how this came to be. Your child then feels that they have to fend for themselves. Maybe they begin borrowing without consultation; maybe they start running up charge cards unbeknownst to you in an attempt to "build their own credit". They may be struggling to find identity, when they really should be enjoying college and focusing on their college coursework. All I want you to do is remember that while these students are your children, they are also on the cusp of adulthood. They need to be encouraged to make thoughtful, rational decisions. As they age and mature, begin to pull back in the academic process so they can navigate their own way.

26

Don't Just Survive, Thrive

Parents, do you realize that many of our students are struggling to just survive the school year? It should come as no surprise given the huge focus we put on coping, surviving & maintaining throughout the long academic year. Between the academic camps, tutoring programs, test preparation sessions and the traditional school months, many kids are in some form of scholarly endeavor most of the calendar year. Some of you may be asking yourself, *what is it that the students are surviving*? I am glad you asked the question. Let's talk brass tax or the real deal– our kids are not looking forward to school like we think they should be. I get the opportunity to meet, coach, mentor & counsel K-12 and college-age students all year long and all over the country. They consistently share that they are bored, disinterested, distracted, fearful, anxiety filled, frustrated, depressed and the list goes on from there.

Before we can even consider discussing academic success, we need to talk about the barriers to student engagement. If your student is not coping with any of the above-mentioned issues, how do you think they will be able to genuinely and willingly participate in the learning process. What I found is that students are trying to figure out how they will navigate the bullying, overcrowded classrooms, constant substitute teachers and lack of quality coursework. Oh yes, they see the same things we see, but they have to deal with it on a regular basis and assess how they will "get along" in the meanwhile.

Consider this book a launching pad for student's academic success. Your household will be turning the corner in how it approaches the process of college preparation and looking at innovative ways all of you can work together progressively. Your progress and program may (probably should) look different than mine – given we are all individual families with unique circumstances – yet, we want similar outcomes, those being students that are: learning, maturing, developing and advancing. We want them reaching to achieve more than we did, and if college is on the horizon, we don't want them to be a casualty of the student loan crisis.

If we are able to allow them the space to be frank and honest, then they may be willing to hear some suggestions on how to not only survive, but thrive in the midst of the school year. This is what we would call a paradigm shift. No longer looking at the year coming with pessimism and a high level of scrutiny, but on the other hand your student could see the possibility of finding benefits in a positive school system filled with quality friendships, learning that aims minds towards future aspirations, clubs, sports and extracurricular activities that unlock hidden potential & untapped interests. This is the picture of an all-together different academic experience. Unfortunately, I believe that our society has associated the aforementioned outlook as reserved for suburban, upper middle class, model students. We have to be careful not to fall into that snare. Each student is entitled to a fair opportunity at having a school experience that causes them to not only come back for more each day, month, year, but it also engages them in multifaceted learning – even when they are expecting it. That, my friends, is THRIVING.

Epilogue:
PAID IN FULL

The date was Wednesday, February 28, 2018, and the final $912 was paid to Spelman College, thus fulfilling the promise that we made to our eldest daughter when she decided to make the Atlanta based historically black college & university (HBCU) her academic home for the previous four years.

Now quiet as kept, that was not the day we thought Spelman would be paid off. I figured we would pay the remaining balance by mid-April (or at least before graduation in May). In keeping with the no loan strategy, the previous 10 months had been extremely tough with both college age daughters attending private universities and living in off-campus apartments requiring large cash outlays every month for rent(s) and the respective tuition payments. Generally speaking, the universities would give you a "financial break" during the May to July timeframe.

During this time, each year, we would try to catch our breath if you will and shift some money to pay other obligations like: taking care of upkeep on the house or a vehicle, or maybe even updating clothing needs for the kids. Whatever the option, there wasn't much wiggle room in those summer months, but "Whew", we could exhale a bit. During this spring semester, "extra" scholarship dollars flowed in. Not much, but it was unexpected funds that allowed us to pay off the final bill a couple months earlier than planned.

What I have just characterized for you represented the previous three years. With both girls in apartments that year and rent due monthly, thus no summer off monetarily. If you add in the security deposit and the first month's rent expenses, you can see why I say those 10 months proved the most challenging financially. There was no down time, no off months, no breather. Was there pressure? For sure, yet with each completed payment, I knew we were one month closer to finishing a four-year, approximately $160K obligation.

Let me take you back to August 2017. There were two tuition payments and two rental payments due for the first time. You could definitely prepare for this by having your money set aside (see chapters on 529, one-income approach, other savings/gifts), so you can pay as you go.

Epilogue: PAID IN FULL

This is essentially a payment plan with the university that you pay each semester's costs over a 4-month time frame. This was part of our strategy. I utilized the full grace period – upwards of 10 days – when paying tuition, as to assist with the household budgeting and getting rental payments ready for the 1st-5th of the month. We always felt good after making the August payment. "Yes!" Remember to celebrate the milestones and mark the occasion. After successfully taking care of the month's obligations, I would send out a group text to my wife and the kids apprising them of the financial update. Keeping them in the loop allowed everyone to remain vested in the family journey to remain debt free while supporting the kid's academic pursuits.

I do need to make an important caveat: there were some snafus on my part along the way. Any miscommunication about bills/obligations between my wife and I could have us scrambling to avoid late fees. Unexpected or unbudgeted expenses could (and did) derail some of my best laid plans. Please be especially careful around the holidays, family travel and the like as these can be cash sinkholes. With our one-income approach you are very much locked into your household budget, given the college expenses are held in the non-household account. On occasion, we needed to attend a wedding or funeral or fix the car, so we were tempted to abandon the process and revert back to our old ways. Please hear me, there were some instances where it felt like we could have borrowed and had more cash on hand, but we were committed as a household to keep pressing. The holidays and birthday celebrations were not as glamorous as prior years, but again we had a difficult goal in mind. Credit cards and loans will seem like viable options – you might even succumb at times – but over the years, I have absolutely seen where finding another way (other than incurring more debt) was the better approach.

Just as we had been on the pay off tuition and apartment leases "kick", we had also been paying down any and all consumer debt (roof & siding repairs, a few retail accounts and travel credit cards). While it was difficult to only pay minimums on accounts for a few years, we kept in constant contact with our creditors. Afterwards, we would send significantly more than what was due, and we were also able to assist and aide others because we were no longer strapped with an overabundance of financial obligations.

So, now what? Well, we had two more children - a daughter who was graduating from Seton Hall University (SHU) in December 2018 (a full semester early), and a son who was graduating high school in June 2019. We would

Epilogue: PAID IN FULL

continue as we had done in previous months/years, we would pay tuition as time went on. In the fall of 2018, we had finished paying for SHU four months before graduation, therefore enabling another daughter to focus on her post, undergraduate life debt free. As for our son, we had been targeting STEM programs and scholarships for years so it was just a matter of deciding on which colleges will make his final list. In the spring of 2019, he decided to go to Drexel University, and the costs were even higher per year than it was for his older sisters. The great news was that the family plan still worked (scholarships and cooperative education opportunities covered almost 75% of the costs). It was even better with just one student in college.

The whole of the college experience [planning for, paying for and celebrating graduations] was an exciting time for our family and friends. I enjoyed sharing our story, and I sincerely hoped that it helps to inform your family's story. Just know this: "...with God all things are possible." Also consider that when we fail to plan, we plan to fail. Remember that everyone's plan for academic success and addressing college costs is slightly different, so be open to exploring the myriad of ways and approaches available to achieving your objectives.

Carpe Diem - Seize the Day

www.ingramcontent.com/pod-product-compliance
Lightning Source LLC
Chambersburg PA
CBHW020911080526
44589CB00011B/536